CONTENTS

Clay Aiken's winning smile is known all over America.

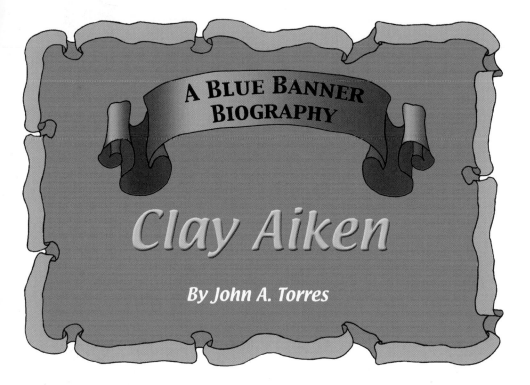

A BLUE BANNER
BIOGRAPHY

Clay Aiken

By John A. Torres

Mitchell Lane
PUBLISHERS

P.O. Box 196
Hockessin, Delaware 19707
Visit us on the web: www.mitchelllane.com
Comments? email us: mitchelllane@mitchelllane.com

Printing   3   4   5   6   7   8   9

Blue Banner Biographies

Alicia Keys	Allen Iverson	Avril Lavigne
Beyoncé	Bow Wow	Britney Spears
Christina Aguilera	Christopher Paul Curtis	**Clay Aiken**
Condoleezza Rice	Daniel Radcliffe	Derek Jeter
Eminem	Eve	Ja Rule
Jay-Z	Jennifer Lopez	J.K. Rowling
Jodie Foster	Lance Armstrong	Mary-Kate and Ashley Olsen
Melissa Gilbert	Michael Jackson	Missy Elliott
Nelly	P. Diddy	Queen Latifah
Ritchie Valens	Rita Williams-Garcia	Ron Howard
Rudy Giuliani	Sally Field	Selena
Shirley Temple		

Library of Congress Cataloging-in-Publication Data
Torres, John Albert
    Clay Aiken / by John A. Torres.
        p. cm. — (A blue banner biography)
    Includes chronology (p.), discography (p.), and index (p.).
    ISBN 1-58415-316-4 (library bound)
        1. Aiken, Clay, 1978 – Juvenile literature. 2. Singers — United States Biography —
Juvenile literature. I. Title. II. Series.
    ML3930.A38T67 2004
    782. 42164'092 – dc22

2004010775

ABOUT THE AUTHOR: John A. Torres is an award-winning journalist covering social issues for *Florida Today Newspaper*. John has also written more than 25 books for various publishers on a variety of topics. He wrote **Marc Anthony**, **Mia Hamm**, and **Fitness Stars of Bodybuilding** for Mitchell Lane Publishers. In his spare time John likes playing sports, going to theme parks, and fishing with his children, step-children and wife, Jennifer.

PHOTO CREDITS: Cover: Getty Images; pp. 4, 8 Getty Images; p. 10 Alec Michael/Globe Photos; pp. 17, 22 Getty Images; p. 28 Fitzroy Barrett/Globe Photos.

Second to None

*I*t may go down as the best second-place finish ever. But on the night of May 20, 2003, it didn't look that way to Clay Aiken. Ruben Studdard had just been announced as the winner of *American Idol* before millions of television viewers. The live theater audience erupted in applause. For a moment, even Ruben looked surprised. Clay put on a smile. The lanky singer was trying his best to look like a good sport. Inside he felt like crying.

Clay and Ruben had outlasted their competition, watching week after week as other contestants were voted off the show. On this final night, it appeared to many viewers as if Ruben sewed up the victory when his velvety singing voice turned to an inspirational gospel music style for "Flying Without Wings." He brought the house down.

Then it was Clay's turn. He chose the old Simon and Garfunkel hit "Bridge Over Troubled Water." The song contains some key changes and some very high notes. Clay would have to be at his absolute best. He had practiced the song over and over again but sometimes it just did not sound right.

> Clay hit the high notes and latched onto the key changes smoothly. He nailed the song "Bridge Over Troubled Water."

For the first time since America saw Clay Aiken, he appeared a bit nervous. Not wishing to make eye contact with the audience, he closed his eyes and started to sing. He hit the melodious high notes and latched onto the key changes smoothly. He nailed it.

Despite the thundering ovation from the crowd, it wasn't enough. Ruben, the burly rhythm and blues singer, left the arena followed by dozens of reporters who wanted to interview him. Only one reporter wanted to talk to Clay.

Normally, the winner's single would be played on the radio weeks or even months before the second-place finisher's. But American Idol judge Simon Cowell—along with other people from the wildly popular television show that lets viewers pick who they think will be the best entertainer—convinced the RCA music company to let both singers put out singles at the same time.

"They were in a sense co-champions, as the numbers had been so close," Cowell said in his book, *I Don't Mean to Be Rude, But….* Out of more than 24 million votes cast nationwide, less than one half of one percent separated the two young men.

Despite his second-place finish on American Idol, Clay's first single went to number one on the music charts. Ruben's only made it to the second spot.

Clay appears on "The Tonight Show With Jay Leno" on January 21, 2004 at the NBC Studios, in Burbank, California.

"Clay Aiken was the ultimate runner-up, underdog," said Kyle Munson, music critic for the *Des Moines Register*, in a personal interview. "His classic vocal styling is more broadly appealing than Ruben's."

How did the skinny kid with the big smile touch America's heart and go from being basically a game show contestant to a mega pop-superstar? That mystery may never be explained, but Cowell had no doubt about Clay's impact.

Clay changed his appearance greatly from the time he started on American Idol.

"I think Clay Aiken has changed American Idol forever," he said in his book. "Six months ago he was a geeky looking kid, working with underprivileged kids and singing for a hobby. Today, Clay Aiken is probably the most talked about singer in America."

After the competition was over and both Clay and Ruben had achieved some measure of stardom, Simon Cowell told them to remember who gave them their opportunity. It was the American public.

It was that same American public that started wanting to know everything there was about Clay Aiken.

Growing Up

Clayton Holmes Aiken was born on November 30, 1978 in Raleigh, North Carolina. From a very young age he displayed a desire to sing and entertain. As soon he could, Clay was walking around his house singing.

Clay was happy and able to sing even though there were some sad and very scary moments when he was a toddler. His biological father was an alcoholic. He sometimes became very violent when he was drinking. He would start arguments with people and curse and cause fights. When he was home he regularly beat Clay's mother, Faye. The beatings became so bad that Clay's mother decided to leave him when Clay was just one year old. That was not so easy. Her husband would track them down and the beatings would start all over again. Fortunately, Clay and his mother finally escaped

Clay with his mother Faye Parker at the 2003 Billboard Music Awards in Las Vegas.

by moving away where they could not be tracked down.

Because Clay loved his mother so much, he did not want anything to do with his biological father. "My mother was beaten by this man and he never tried to be a father to me, ever," Clay said in a telephone interview. "We moved so he wouldn't know where I was."

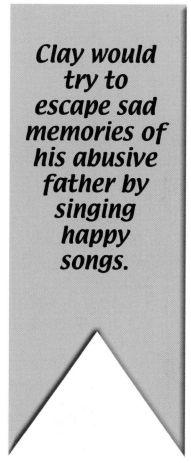

Clay would try to escape sad memories of his abusive father by singing happy songs.

Clay had been born as Clayton Grissom, his biological father's last name. He disliked that name so much that he changed it to Aiken, his mother's maiden name, in 1999.

When he and his mother were not moving around to escape an abusive man, Clay was busy grabbing hairbrushes or rolling up magazines and singing into them, even though he was only a few years old. "Clay was always the entertainer," his mother told Jennifer Wulff of *People* magazine. "Give him anything that looked like a microphone and he'd perform."

Always the entertainer, Clay would try to escape the sad memories of his father by singing happy songs and telling lots of jokes. He recalled that he always dressed up as a clown for Halloween when he was a child. He liked clowns because he felt they brought joy to children. His mother said that one Halloween, Clay dressed as Raggedy Andy. Clay politely disagreed. He insisted that he was always a clown.

Before Clay turned three, he became a singer. Not only was he a singer, he was also the family ham.

Mother and son are in complete agreement about one thing during Clay's younger days: Even before he turned three, he became a singer. "I've been singing forever," he told Jennifer Wulff. "I think that's pretty appropriate."

Clay was not just a singer. He was also the family ham. Clay loved it whenever the attention was put on him. He would regularly imitate Santa Claus as a little boy and ask people what they wanted for Christmas. He would then reach into his imaginary bag of goodies and dole out make-believe gifts. It was even better if someone had a camera. Clay would pose and mug for the photographer as well as make funny faces and do impersonations.

When Clay turned seven, he and his mother decided he should show his talents to a wider audience.

He tried out for a county production. He chose to sing the song "Yankee Doodle Dandy," made famous decades earlier by legendary actor and entertainer James Cagney. Clay practiced every chance he could but it was not enough. He did not make the audition.

That didn't stop Clay from singing and performing for family and friends. With enough practice he started to pass auditions. He began performing in local theaters, talent shows, church choirs, and school plays.

Clay's stepfather Ray promised to protect Clay from his abusive biological father.

During this time, Clay's mother fell in love with a good man by the name of Ray Parker. After the marriage, Ray became Clay's stepfather and promised to protect the family from Clay's biological father. Clay began to forget the nightmares that his biological father had caused the family. He grew to love Ray Parker. Before long he was calling him "Dad." Unfortunately, Ray never got to see Clay's rise to fame and fortune. He passed away in 2002.

Before his death, he had plenty of chances to see and hear Clay sing. Both Ray and Faye worked at Sears department store. Sometimes Clay would stand on the counter and sing country songs. He was also a member of the Raleigh Boys Choir and sang at the Leesville Road Baptist Church.

In 1995, when Clay was 16, he won the starring role in Leesville Road High School's production of the famous musical play *Oklahoma*. To this day, Clay laughs when he sees photos of himself dressed up in the cowboy-type costume for the show. "I didn't just go around dressed up like that all the time," he told Jennifer Wulff.

Clay loved to sing and perform, but never thought he would become a professional singer.

Even though Clay never thought that he would become a professional singer, he knew one thing clearly enough. He thoroughly enjoyed being the center of attention when he was performing. "I just love going up and singing on stage," he said to Joan Anderman of the *Boston Globe*.

Little did he suspect where that love would take him.

Helping Kids

*C*lay Aiken loved to sing and perform from a young age. There was no doubt about that. But Clay also knew the incredible, almost impossible, odds that faced any singer hoping to make it big.

So he considered singing and performing simply as a hobby. He had no intention of making it a career. He decided early on what sort of career he did want to have. It would be something that involved helping children. Maybe this choice had to do with his experiences as a youngster with an abusive father. He wanted to become a teacher. But not just an ordinary teacher. Clay wanted to become a special education teacher and work with kids who had special needs. "I enjoy singing. I love performing," he said to Leigh Dyer and Mark Johnson of the *Charlotte Observer*. But there's a completely different kind of thrill when you work with kids."

Fortunately, Clay was blessed with the patience and good humor that a person needs to be a teacher. He is also very energetic and very positive, more attributes of successful teachers.

Clay's life would change forever during his summer internship in Raleigh, North Carolina.

So, after he graduated from high school in 1997, Clay entered the University of North Carolina at Charlotte and began working to earn his teaching degree.

"I had my life planned out for me," Clay said. "I was going to be a teacher. I once worked three months to get a child to be able to read a word. You don't get anyone clapping for you when you do that. You work hard and you earn it," he explained to Joan Anderman.

Clay's life would change forever when he worked on a summer internship in Raleigh. He was tutoring and helping a 13-year-old boy named Michael. Michael was autistic. He had withdrawn into his own private world.

When Clay was with Michael, he would often talk and joke about being on television. He especially liked

The Amazing Race. He even told Michael's mother, Diane Bubel, that he wanted to try out for the program.

She had other ideas. Sometimes Clay brought over a laptop computer filled with songs he had written. But Bubel did not want to see those songs; she wanted to

Clay attends the World Children's Day at McDonalds on November 20, 2003 in Los Angeles, California.

hear them. She asked Clay to sing. "And he started singing," Bubel said during an appearance on the *Oprah Winfrey Show*. "So, anytime we'd have a conversation about music he'd just start singing, and we were like 'Wow!'"

Soon Diane Bubel convinced Clay that he should audition for a new television show. It was *American Idol*. The highly successful show was a spinoff from a similar program in England.

> Diane Bubel convinced Clay to audition for American Idol.

Clay wore a WWJD (What Would Jesus Do?) bracelet on his wrist. He put the decision into God's hands. Clay said wearing the bracelet is a reminder of God and the amount of trust and faith he has in Him. After all, singing was easy for Clay. Maybe God had a different plan for him than teaching. If the singing failed, he could go back to teaching. That was what he had planned to do anyway.

"I didn't work hard to be able to sing," he told Joan Anderman. "God gave that to me. It's easy, and people scream and cheer, and who wouldn't like that? It's great."

Clay drove to Charlotte, North Carolina for the *American Idol* tryouts, but he failed to impress the judges. Clay refused to give up. He auditioned a second time in Atlanta, Georgia and sang his heart out so he wouldn't be sent home. This time he was successful. He sang "Always and Forever," by the 1970s group Heatwave.

Clay knew that his voice probably wouldn't be enough to impress the tough judges once the show made it to Hollywood. That wasn't the only problem. Cowell — who has a reputation for speaking his mind — told Clay that he didn't look like a pop star.

At the American Idol audition Clay didn't look like a pop star.

Clay decided to lose his eyeglasses in favor of contact lenses. He traded in his typical clothes for something more flashy. He even changed his hairstyle and dyed his brown hair red. A friend of his mother helped him dye his hair the first time but it turned blue. Clay joked that he looked like an old lady.

Now he had new clothes, new eyes and new hair. Would it be enough to impress America?

Idol

On January 21, 2003, the second season of *American Idol* telecasts began. Just eight days later Clay made it to the next round. He was one of only 32 finalists. The show had started with 234 contestants!

The finalists were divided into four groups of eight each. Clay's next performance was on February 11. He sang the rock ballad "Open Arms," by Journey. The fans and judges liked the performance. The television viewers didn't. Clay was eliminated. Only two singers from his group were chosen to remain. They were Ruben Studdard and Kimberley Locke.

Instead of going home happy with the experience, Clay decided to compete for what is called a "wild card" spot. Viewers and judges could bring back contestants who had been voted off and give them a second chance.

Several weeks later, Clay sang the Elton John classic, "Don't Let the Sun Go Down on Me." The fans loved it. They lit up the switchboards and Clay got more telephone votes than anybody else. He was back on the show! So were three others whom the judges brought back.

American Idol fans loved it when Clay sang Elton John's "Don't Let the Sun Go Down on Me."

Now Clay was among the final 12 singers. For the next 10 weeks, he would be facing possible elimination every time he sang. One contestant would be voted off every time until just two remained and the new American Idol would be selected.

The next few competitions were tricky. Clay had to pick music from certain categories. For example, he picked the Four Tops classic "I Can't Help Myself," for Motown night. For movie music night, Clay picked "Somewhere Out There," from the animated film *An American Tail*. He survived. Two other contestants didn't. They were voted off.

Clay is most at home singing romantic ballads that the whole family can enjoy.

Clay was starting to taste the feeling of success. Although he kept telling family and friends that he would just go home and finish his college degree if he didn't "make it" on *American Idol*, he felt like anything could happen now.

It was around this time that Americans began to really identify with Clay Aiken. After all, he was skinny and wholesome and said things like "y'all" and "dang." He called himself "dorky" and a "geek." He even admitted that his idol had always been Mr. Rogers, the children's television show host known for his conservative sweaters. Soon he became the fan favorite.

Americans identified with Clay because he was skinny and had a wholesome personality.

By the end of March, Clay even had Cowell convinced. Known as the toughest judge on the show, Cowell told a national entertainment magazine that if he was a betting man, he would be putting his money on Clay Aiken to win the competition.

On April 1, Clay sang "Everlasting Love" for his disco number. It was clear that disco was not his strength. His performance was only mediocre. No one knows if he would have been voted off that night.

Instead, the show decided to eliminate a singer who had just been arrested for assault. For his number 1 hit selection the following week, Clay sang "At This Moment" by Billy Vera and the Beaters. This is a very emotional love song that was featured on the 1980s Michael J. Fox sitcom, *Family Ties*. Clay sang it with just the right amount of emotion and intensity.

Clay was starting to attract the attention of record company executives who watch and attend the show. They consider not just vocal talent but also how the public responds to the entertainer's personality. They liked what they saw in Clay.

"There are plenty of singers with great voices and great pop songs, but Clay has a really down-to-earth personality," Steve Ferrera, a record company executive, explained to Joan Anderman. "He's completely grounded and absolutely likable and people see that."

Clay's next performance was the upbeat "Tell Her About It," by Billy Joel. With yet another competitor removed from the show, he was one of six remaining. Lurking in Clay's mind through all this was the fact that Ruben Studdard and Kimberley Locke—the two singers who had beaten him in the earlier competition—were still around. Ruben and Kimberley were singing great songs and winning fans and judges, too. Maybe Clay thought they would beat him again. Maybe he thought third place was the best he could hope for.

A True Idol

*B*y the time Clay Aiken had advanced this far into the competition, the folks from his home state of North Carolina were genuinely excited. The fans couldn't keep away from their television sets. Many of them were starting to believe that he really had a chance to win. Even the governor wanted to meet him.

Their excitement had another source. Clay talked about turning his fame into helping others if he won. He was interested in starting a foundation for disabled kids and continuing his work with autistic children. Clay was a genuine person. When he was told that he could make a lot more money if he started writing songs, Clay simply answered that he loved singing and was not so interested in the money.

His next two appearances were in front of Diane Warren and Neil Sedaka, two very well known and respected songwriters. Clay impressed Warren when he sang her composition "I Could Not Ask for More." And he totally blew away Sedaka, one of his favorite songwriters, with "Build Me Up Buttercup" and then the sad Sedaka classic, "Solitaire."

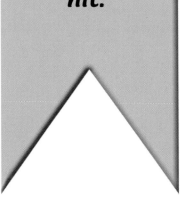

Even though Clay was dissappointed at finishing second he got to record a CD with a #1 hit.

Simon Cowell, the sharp-tongued judge, had nothing but good things to say after hearing Clay's version of "Solitaire." He called it a fantastic performance. Even Sedaka could not believe his ears. After the show he told reporters that he would love to produce Clay's CD if he ever got to record one.

A week later, on May 6, Clay sang a couple of Bee Gees songs, "To Love Somebody" and "Grease." When the votes were tallied, it was down to Clay and Ruben and Kimberley. Clay went home to North Carolina. He was honored as a hero. He met Governor Mike Easley and sang the national anthem before a minor league baseball game.

The rest is history. Voting the following week narrowed the competition to Clay and Ruben. Even though he was disappointed in finishing second, Clay got to record a CD and had a number-one hit record. Despite the competition and the fact that Clay's record made it to number one, he and Ruben became friends. They began talking on the phone to see how each other was doing.

Clay headlined several musical tours after the show. His debut album, *Measure of A Man*, sold 613,000 copies in the first week following its release in October, 2003. It topped the charts for months, was later certified platinum and has sold more than two million copies. While critics did not give rave reviews to the album, many agreed that the boyish-faced singer had a great voice, tremendous appeal and would be around for a very long, long time. Former classmates began selling school yearbooks, photos and videotapes of old talent shows featuring Clay on the Internet, which furthered his appeal.

Despite the American Idol competition Clay and Ruben became friends.

True to his word, Clay used his newfound fame and money to help others. He started the Bubel/Aiken Foundation for Children with Disabilities. He also remained true to himself when he defied the record company and refused to sing any songs that had suggestive or offensive lyrics. He even stopped shooting the video for his first single, "This is the Night," because he did not like what the record company wanted him to do. "I've got a responsibility to

Clay at the 2003 American Music Awards where he received the Fans Choice Award.

the public," Clay said to Joan Anderman. "Parents want to let their kids listen to people they can trust."

An Arizona man named Todd Venice started an online fan club for Clay. Within a few weeks the club had more than 5,000 members. Venice had a good explanation for Clay's appeal. "Clay touches the geek in all of us," he told Nick Marino of the *Atlanta Journal-Constitution*. "We watched him blossom, like a flower almost. His first appearance on *American Idol* was so the opposite of a pop star. You could never imagine him being a sex symbol—it was just the opposite."

> *Even today Clay is still not comfortable with his fame. But he knows to enjoy it because it could be fleeting.*

Even today Clay is still not exactly comfortable with his fame. He told VH-1 in an interview that he wished he could still just go to a supermarket and buy some groceries. But he also knew enough to enjoy the fame because it may be fleeting. "I do my best to try and remember this is a once in a lifetime thing, love it, live it up and enjoy it because next year they may not want you," he explained.

Anyone who has heard him sing knows he's wrong. Clay Aiken is here to stay.

CHRONOLOGY

1978	Born on November 30
1981	Shows a love of singing at the age of two and a half
1983	Starts doing impersonations, including his favorite, Santa Claus
1985	Auditions for a county production but does not get the part
1995	Stars in his high school production of *Oklahoma*
1997	Enrolls at the University of North Carolina at Charlotte, intending to become a special education teacher
2002	Auditions for *American Idol*
2003	Places second in the *American Idol* finals
2003	First single, "This is the Night/Bridge Over Troubled Water," makes it to number one on the charts
2003	Releases first album, *Measure of a Man*
2003	Wins *Fans Choice Award* at the *American Music Awards*
2003	Wins Bestselling Single of the Year for *This is the Night/ Bridge Over Troubled Water* at the *Billboard* Music Awards
2003	Graduates from UNC Charlotte in December
2004	Begins a singing tour throughout America

FOR FURTHER READING

Books

Aiken, Clay. *Learning to Sing: Hearing the Music in Your Life.* New York: Random House, 2004.

Tracy, Kathleen. *From Second Place to the Top of the Charts.* Hockessin, Delaware: Mitchell Lane Publishers, 2004.

Cowell, Simon. *I Don't Mean to Be Rude, But...* New York: Broadway Books, 2003.

News Articles

Anderman, Joan. "The Voice of a Star, the Soul of a Nerd." *Boston Globe*, March 10, 2004.

Cohen, Howard. "Here Comes Mr. American Idol." *Miami Herald*, Feb. 27, 2004.

Deggans, Eric. "America Loves a Runner-up." *St. Petersburg Times*, Feb. 26, 2004.

Devores, Courtney. "Clay Shines in City he Called Home." *Charlotte Observer*, Feb. 25, 2004.

Hay, Carla. "The Measure of a Rising Star." *Billboard Magazine*, Feb. 23, 2004.

"All I Have to Do is Dream," *People* Magazine, May 2003.

"Clay Aiken's Rise to Fame," *The News & Observer*, May 23, 2003.

On the Internet
Offical Website
> http://www.clayaiken.com

The Bubel/Aiken Foundation
> http://www.thebubelaikenfoundation.org

2003   *Measure of a Man* (album) RCA
2003   *Bridge Over Troubled Water/This is the Night* (single) RCA
2003   *Solitare/Invisible* (single) RCA
2003   *Invisible*   (single) RCA
2004   *Way/Solitaire* (RCA)